FLOODS!

by Ellen Keller

SCHOLASTIC INC.
New York Toronto London Auckland Sydney
Mexico City New Delhi Hong Kong

ACKNOWLEDGMENTS
The publisher is grateful to the following for
permission to reproduce their photographs:

Cover and photo insert: AP/Wide World Photo, FEMA,
Army Corps of Engineers, National Weather Service

Special thanks to the following for permission to use the
first-hand accounts found in chapter six: Betsey Palmiscno
and Gregory Knoblock

No part of this publication may be reproduced in whole or in part,
or stored in a retrieval system, or transmitted in any form or by any
means, electronic, mechanical, photocopying, recording, or otherwise,
without written permission of the publisher. For information regarding
permission, write to Simon Spotlight, an imprint of Simon & Schuster
Children's Publishing Division, 1230 Avenue of the Americas,
New York, NY 10020.

ISBN 0-439-27082-0

Copyright © 1999 by The Weather Channel, Inc. All rights reserved.
Published by Scholastic Inc., 555 Broadway, New York, NY 10012,
by arrangement with Simon Spotlight, an imprint of Simon & Schuster
Children's Publishing Division. "The Weather Channel" is a registered
trademark of The Weather Channel, Inc. used under license.
SCHOLASTIC and associated logos are trademarks and/or
registered trademarks of Scholastic Inc.

12 11 10 9 8 7 6 5   5 6/0

Printed in the U.S.A.   23

First Scholastic printing, March 2001

Contents

Chapter 1	The Great Flood of 1997	7
Chapter 2	Reasons for Floods	16
Chapter 3	River Floods	27
Chapter 4	Fear in a Flash	38
Chapter 5	Other Types of Floods	45
Chapter 6	Real Safety/Real People	50
Glossary		61
Index		63

1

The Great Flood of 1997

You've heard the words **natural disaster**. They can describe an earthquake, a tornado, or any other force of nature that causes destruction. A flood can be a natural disaster, too. Life is hard for victims of a flood. People talk and think about nothing else. But they find comfort in the words of their neighbors: "We're in this together. We belong to a community. We watch out for each other. It will be all right."

That's what happened to many kids who

lived in and around Grand Forks, North Dakota, and East Grand Forks, Minnesota, before the Great Flood of 1997. As the Red River rose, more and more neighborhoods were evacuated. Families lived in shelters or slept on floors in the homes of relatives and friends. During the day, older kids went back to their neighborhoods to work on the **dikes** alongside their parents and other families. Everyone worked. Everyone worried. What was going to happen?

What happened was the worst flood ever of the Red River. Before it was over flood waters, melting snow, and oozing mud claimed many of the homes and neighborhoods surrounding the river. Some families had to move across town. Some moved to other places to begin life again. Why was the flood of 1997 so bad? It was because of what happened previously, in the winter and early spring of 1997.

Like many places in the United States that year, towns and cities in western Minnesota and Eastern North Dakota had one of the worst winters on record. The area in and around Grand Forks, North Dakota, was pummeled with seven different **blizzards**. Before it was over, about one hundred inches of snow had fallen. Buildings were crushed under the weight. Cattle and other farm animals froze to death. Snowdrifts in some places grew taller than ten feet.

Everywhere, there was talk of melting snow and the floods to come. But the people who had grown up near the water believed they could handle the river. They were tough.

And then in the beginning of April, one last furious blizzard slammed in. It began with freezing rain, which changed to sleet and then snow with hurricane-strength winds. In areas near the Red River, 300,000 people lost their electricity.

Everyone knew what was coming. No one could guess how bad it would be. First the Minnesota River rose dangerously on its way to meet the Red River. People in Minnesota worked feverishly to build up the dikes. The people along the Red River in Grand Forks, North Dakota, filled **sandbags** to make the dike stronger and higher. The government spent millions of dollars for emergency dikes, pumps, and other equipment for nineteen communities along the Red and Minnesota Rivers. Men, women, and children worked together to save their towns.

Leaving Home

On the night of Friday, April 18, the people of Grand Forks were awakened by sirens piercing the darkness, signaling everyone to get up from their beds and leave their homes.

The dike broke. The water rushed into the city. It moved up streets and into backyards. It flooded the beautiful old homes along the river, covering them with water up to the roofs.

Portions of Grand Forks, North Dakota, and East Grand Forks, Minnesota, were deluged with water. The river had entered over 11,000 homes and businesses. Some people knew the situation was hopeless, so they closed their doors and walked away hoping they would have something to come back to. Rescuers paddled boats up and down streets looking for people who hadn't gotten out in time.

Silence and Smell

By the next day, Saturday, many neighborhoods in Grand Forks were completely silent and abandoned. About half of Grand Forks, North Dakota, was flooded. Almost all of East Grand Forks, Minnesota, was filled with water.

Later people would say one of the most memorable aspects of the flood in Grand Forks was the terrible smell. The water had not only invaded the streets and yards, it

> **Did You Know?**
>
> The Emergency Animal Rescue Service and the Humane Society worked hard during The Great Flood of 1997 rescuing animals both wild and domestic. Animals may be injured while trying to escape flood waters. They may also starve if their food source has been cut off, or become dehydrated because they are unable to drink the polluted flood waters.

had crashed into the underground sewage system and entered the toilets and bathtubs. The stench of the city's waste filled the air, along with the smell of half-used paint and fuel oil cans that had been stored in thousands of basements.

And still the river kept rising. The National Weather Service predicted that the Red River would **crest** the next day. By afternoon, four feet of water covered much of downtown Grand Forks. Other parts of the dike began to break. The National Guard and the citizens worked frantically to repair it.

Just when everyone thought it couldn't get any worse, it did. On Saturday afternoon, the dike broke in new places.

Fire on Water

Fire! It began in the Security Building in downtown Grand Forks. It resulted from wet electrical wires. Before it was over, the fire tore through eleven buildings and three city blocks.

Before firefighters could even begin their work, they had to evacuate about forty apartment dwellers who had refused to leave their homes when the orders were given. After the people were rescued, the fire fighting began. Planes hovered overhead dropping chemical retardant on burning buildings. Some firefighters tried in vain to hook up hoses to underwater hydrants. Many of the fire trucks couldn't get through the four feet of water covering the streets.

The fire burned through the night and into the next afternoon. The employees of the newspaper, *The Grand Forks Herald*, abandoned their building and set up temporary offices in a school out of the flood zone. The newspaper men and women never stopped working. The citizens needed them, and the news and information they could deliver were now more important than ever. People left messages at the newspaper. They offered people without homes places to stay. They asked for news of missing relatives. *The Grand Forks Herald* was able to comfort and help many people. A year later, in 1998, the paper received a great honor, the Pulitzer Prize.

The Community Rebuilds

Finally the flood and the fire were over. New sounds filled the air. Hovering helicopters brought the president of the United States to survey the damage. Heavy trucks and other machinery roared as workers tore down buildings and built new ones. Some families settled back into their old neighborhoods. Others made friends in new places.

One year later, in April of 1998, the people of Grand Forks and East Grand Forks planned a flood anniversary. Despite all the devastation and hardship, there was one thing almost everyone agreed on. The sense of community and friendship had never been as great as it was during the flood. Strangers became friends. The anniversary was a celebration of the spirit of caring that was invoked by the flood and the hope for the future.

2

Reasons for Floods

Here's something surprising to think about: Since the beginning of time, the earth has always had the same water in the same amount. Have you ever heard someone say, "Hell-o! What's that you're drinking from the water fountain? Watch out! It could be recycled dinosaur spit!"

That may be an exaggeration, but the fact remains: the amount of water on and around the earth is always the same. It doesn't ever change!

Three-fourths of the earth is covered with water. To see that, all you need to do is look at a globe. Water is found in oceans, lakes, rivers, streams, rain forests and swamps—it's even found in water-filled ditches beside the road. Water is everywhere. You can even find water in the desert if you look hard enough.

So why do we have floods in some years and not in others? Weather is one answer. Rain, snow, and violent storms are part of it. The ground's ability to soak up moisture is part of it, too. And people also play a big part; where they live, what they build.

> **Did You Know?**
>
> The **atmosphere** is a mass of gases that surrounds planet Earth and extends several hundred miles above the surface. Weather is created by unequal heating of Earth's surface by the sun which causes air and moisture to move about within the atmosphere. Floods from heavy rains or snowmelt begin in the atmosphere.

Floods from Rain and Melting Snow

Floods are waters that spill out and cover land that is usually dry. Forms of **precipitation** such as heavy rain or snow are the greatest cause of flooding.

You can probably remember a spring season when it rained for many days straight. It doesn't happen every year, but when it does, these conditions are right for a flood. In areas where there is a heavy winter snowfall, spring can bring melting snow and heavy flooding. For instance, in the winter before the Great Flood of 1997, eight blizzards dropped one hundred inches of snow on the area around Grand Forks, North Dakota.

Does that mean there is more water on and above the earth when it floods? No, the amount of water is always the same but it is not always in the same places. Much of Earth's water is stored in oceans, rivers, lakes, glaciers, springs, and other underground areas. Over time, water from these evaporates, then turns into clouds and eventually to precipitation. This is called the water cycle. When a large amount of water appears as rain or snow in one place, there may be a flood.

> **Did You Know?**
>
> Masses of warm air and cold air move over the land causing different weather, including rain. Sometimes the leading edge of a warm or a cold air mass, called a front, stalls over a particular land area. Then there may be an unusual amount of rain.

All water is part of a never-ending cycle, no matter where that water is found. Imagine a puddle on the sidewalk in front of your house, for example:

- The sun beats down on the puddle.

- The warmth of the sun helps the water to evaporate creating a gas called water **vapor**. The puddle slowly disappears.

- This water vapor continues to rise through the atmosphere joining other water vapors—maybe from oceans or rivers. As the water vapor rises, it mixes with salt from the sea, tiny grains of soil, and smoke particles. Eventually the temperature cools enough that the water vapor condenses onto the tiny grains of salt and smoke, forming liquid water drops and creating a cloud. Some clouds are light and fleecy. Some are huge weighing many thousands of tons.

- From these clouds comes rain (and sleet or snow if the air is cold enough). Some of this precipitation drops to the ground. Some may become another puddle in front of your house. Then the cycle begins again.

Ground Saturation Contributes to Floods

As rain falls and snow melts, water sinks deeper and deeper into the earth. It soaks through soil and porous rock. It fills the roots of trees, grass, and other plants.

Water rises in springs, holes, and through any empty spaces underground. Then there comes a point when this water, called **groundwater**, hits solid rock deep under the earth and it can't sink any further.

The ground above the solid rock fills with water. The soil is soaked or **saturated**. The tree roots and underground water passages can't absorb any more water. Puddles appear on top of the ground. Extra water runs off the land into any available bodies of water such as rivers and lakes. The water in rivers and lakes rises.

Some land surfaces can more easily absorb tremendous amounts of water. In places where the hard rock is deep in the earth and covered with many feet of rich soil, a lot of water can be absorbed. If the soil is made up mostly of clay, not much water can soak in. In places where solid rock is close to the surface or on the surface, such as on mountains or in canyons, the ground cannot absorb much water at all.

To understand ground saturation, imagine you've spilled a large pan of water on the floor. A dry sponge will soak up a lot of water. But when the sponge is filled, or saturated, it cannot hold any more of the water spill. The water leaks out of the sponge back onto the floor. The same thing happens with saturated ground. The ground water leaks out to form puddles and streams which run off into rivers, lakes, and oceans.

Try This
What is the ground like in your garden, your yard, or a nearby park?

Can it soak up water? How fast? Make a soil saturation device and use it to check out the land in your area in two or three different places.

1. Have an adult help you cut off both ends of a can to create your soil saturation device.

2. Choose a spot—maybe in your back yard. Push one end of the can into the soil about a half inch deep.

3. Quickly fill the can with water.

4. Time it to see how long it takes for the water to completely drain out of the can.

5. Do this again in another area and compare the drainage times. Which land can absorb more water? Why do you think that is?

6. Try using your device before it rains

and after it rains. Compare the different drainage times. Repeat your experiment in a different area. Before you pour the water, try to predict the drainage time.

PEOPLE BUILD AND THE FLOODS COME

A third major factor that contributes to flooding is the way people make use of the land. Many farms, towns, and cities have been built near water. Since the days of the pioneers, boats were used to ship food and other supplies. People used rivers and lakes for drinking water, fishing, cooking, bathing, and washing clothes. To this day, people like to live along a river or near a lake because it is so beautiful. But people living next to bodies of water can cause problems.

Rivers and lakes naturally overflow every so often. The surrounding land onto which they spill is called a **floodplain**.

People who live in the floodplain are in the direct path of the natural flooding process. Some people want to farm the rich and fertile soil. Others simply want to live in towns and cities on the river. Space taken up by houses and whole towns leaves less space for overflowing river water. So people build dams and dikes to keep the water inside the banks of the rivers.

But the water has to go somewhere. It will have to flood in other places now that part of it is dammed up. So upstream or downstream, the floods may come.

There are many families who have lived through floods from one year to the next and from generation to generation. They know the floods are coming. They move their furniture and valuables to the top floors in their houses. These families cannot imagine moving away. This is where they've always lived and this is where they will stay.

Other families feel differently. Living through floods is hard, and rebuilding damaged homes again and again wears people down. These people apply to the government for individual families or whole communities to move their towns to higher ground, out of reach of floods. The floodplain lands are then left as parks people can enjoy when the ground is not flooded.

> **Did You Know?**
>
> The government will buy houses from people living in the floodplains. The people can then take the money and build new homes away from the flood area.

3

River Floods

People will tell you that the most frightening thing about a natural disaster is the element of surprise. Tornadoes, for instance, come with little warning. A river flood, on the other hand, can occur gradually—over days, weeks, or even months. Scientists look at the weather and the land saturation. They measure the rising water. Slowly, a disaster in the making becomes big news. People watch and wait. They worry. How bad will it be this time?

River floods are by far the biggest and most damaging type of flood. When you hear about floods in coastal states, you may think the cause is the ocean, and sometimes it is. But more often it is the rivers. It could be the Napa River in California or the Willamette River in Oregon. It might be the Kennebec River in Maine or any river in any state whether it is on the ocean or not.

> **Did You Know?**
>
> The tiniest river is called a creek but it can expand and become a powerful and damaging force. In June 1998, after what people described as a month's worth of rain in twenty-four hours, the Ochoco Creek in Prineville, Oregon, swept through the town of 5,400 people, damaging about 400 homes and completely destroying others.

When expanding creeks or huge rivers like the Mississippi rise, so does the power of the water. As it races along, confined in the space between river banks, the water gathers great pressure, especially at the bottom. Whirlpools can occur. The moving water gouges and scrapes the sides and the bed of the river. It drags with it mud, rocks, tree trunks, old tires, and other **debris** from people's lives. This all contributes to the tremendous weight of the water. When a river bursts its banks, it can race on for miles and the damage can be great.

Ice-jam Floods

Imagine a dam of ice in a river that is so high and so strong that dynamite is needed to blast it out. This type of damming can occur in the Ohio Valley, in New York state, and in many other parts of the northern United States.

Here is how it can happen. Heavy snow falls often. Ice forms on the river and thickens throughout the winter. Then, all at once, warm temperatures settle over the land and the river. Heavy rain falls on the melting snow. The river ice breaks apart, sometimes in chunks so huge they can drag a barn or a house with them. The ice and debris move downstream. At a bend in the river or a bridge or a dam, the ice chunks jam closer together. The water stops. It can't get through. It plunges over the river banks, over the roads and yards, and into the first and second floors of homes.

> **Did You Know?**
>
> Warning of an ice-jam flood comes from insects called snow fleas. These tiny fleas hatch and crawl up along ice-covered river banks, moving toward the sun. When people see them, usually the ice chunks will start to flow within four to seven days.

The Mississippi River Basin

Throughout history, river floods have produced some of the worst natural disasters. Many of these have happened in the area known as the Mississippi River Basin.

The Mississippi, one of the great rivers of the world, cuts a path from Minnesota to the Gulf of Mexico. Water from an amazing 100,000 rivers, creeks, and streams flows into the Mississippi River. These 100,000 rivers, creeks, and streams are called **tributaries**.

The land that the Mississippi and its tributaries flow through is called the Mississippi River Basin. This basin contains the wetlands, floodplains, fertile farming soil, towns, and cities that the Mississippi and its tributaries can reach if water rises and a flood comes.

Millions of people live near the Mississippi and its tributaries. These people and the government have built miles of dikes to hold back flood waters. Yet some part of the basin floods almost every year. When there is great rainfall or snowmelt over the Mississippi River Basin, the Mississippi River rises. As a result, some of those rivers, or the Mississippi itself, will overflow.

> **Did You Know?**
>
> Some families who live in the floodplain over many generations have no plans to move. Many houses have pegs on the walls of the first floor where they can hang their furniture to protect it from the flood waters.

The Mississippi River:

- is 2,348 miles long.
- begins as a small creek at Itaska in northern Minnesota.
- ends at the Gulf of Mexico.
- gets its water from about 100,000 rivers and streams.
- has one tributary, the Missouri River, which is slightly longer at 2,533 miles.

Kids do important work by piling sandbags to hold back the flood waters in the Midwest.

Filling sandbags is a tough job but these kids and adults work together to get it done.

Even buses have trouble getting through this flooded street.

(NOAA)

Water continues to rise and floods this house.

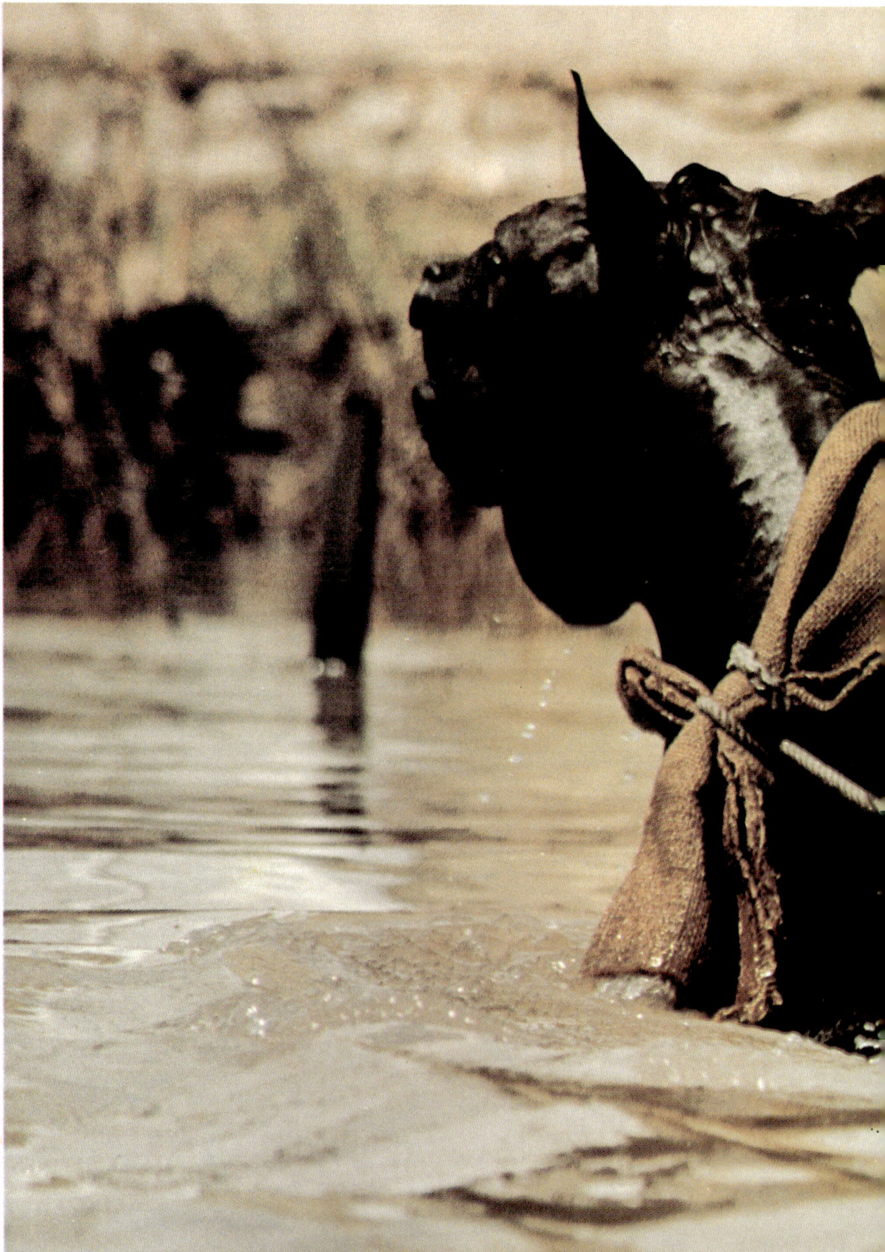

A veterinarian rides a horse out of flood waters to safety.

Animal rescue workers bring food and help to a cow in danger.

Extensive damage is caused to plantlife during flooding.

Even a puppy gets rescued.

With flood waters rising, even this guardhouse was abandoned.

Flood waters travel up tree trunks and up the pole holding this sign.

> **THE MISSISSIPPI RIVER BASIN:**
> - covers parts of thirty-one states and two Canadian provinces.
> - covers more than a million square miles of land and rivers.

The Great Flood of 1993

June and July can be hot, dusty months in Kansas and Missouri, but not in 1993. In the upper Mississippi River Basin, heavy rains fell in April and continued on through July. Parts of Iowa, Illinois, Nebraska, Minnesota, Wisconsin, and North and South Dakota were deluged with twice as much rainfall as is normal. In some places, rainfall was heavier than it had been in one hundred years. A great flood was in the making.

> **Did You Know?**
>
> Some people called the Flood of 1993 a 500-year-flood. That means that there is only a one in 500 chance (in a given year) that a flood that size could happen.

As summer wore on, rain drenched the upper Mississippi River Basin. Fourteen rivers, including the Mississippi, Ohio, and Missouri, reached crests that had never been seen before. Relentless rain fell from June 1 to August 1, in some spots four to five times the average amount. More than one hundred rivers overflowed their banks and raced across the farmlands, towns, and cities of the Upper Midwest. Nearly three hundred government-built dikes were breached as the water broke through or raced over them.

There were other dikes built by the farmers and townspeople. Men, women, and teenagers worked frantically to strengthen the dikes they had built and maintained for so many years. But in many areas, the floods came anyway. Before it was over, the Great Flood of 1993 would affect parts of nine states, cause $12 billion in damage, and result in the loss of forty-eight human lives.

The Great Flood of 1927

In 1927, a huge flood was building in the lower Mississippi River Basin that would later be called the greatest natural disaster this country has ever known. It was April, and there had been heavy rain since January in the middle Mississippi River Basin. Tributaries had already flooded. Down on the lower Mississippi River, towns such as Memphis, New Orleans, and Greenville, Mississippi, watched and worried.

At night people lay in their beds and listened to the pounding of the river as it roared in its banks on its way south to the ocean. Workers fought frantically to strengthen the dikes as the water rose from the rain and the flooding up north. Out on the river overturned boats and whole trees were sucked under by the current and then shot into the air like fired missiles.

And then the Mississippi River broke free from its banks and raced over 26,000 square miles between the months of April and June. Close to a million people were forced to leave their homes. Almost a thousand people were said to have died. The Red Cross fed about 700,000 refugees for many months. This flood gave new meaning to the word "disaster."

Did You Know?

In the Great Flood of 1993, the part of the Mississippi below the Missouri River carried one million cubic feet of water per second. In 1927, a week after the flood in Greenville, MS, the river carried three million cubic feet of water per second.

The Army Corps of Engineers

After the terrible flood of 1927, the president of the United States established the Army Corps of Engineers. One of its most important tasks is to work to diminish flood damage. Today the Army Corps of Engineers build tunnels, bridges, roads, and buildings to make life better and easier for people in flood zones, while helping to preserve the environment. There have been many serious floods since the Corps was established, but floods would probably have been much more frequent and much worse were it not for the work of the Corps.

4

Fear in a Flash

River waters can rise slowly from melting snow or heavy summer rainfall. Sometimes it takes months for a river to build to flood stage, burst out of its banks, and devour the land. But there is another kind of flood. It is called a **flash flood**. It is destructive. Flash floods are sudden and difficult to predict.

A flash flood can happen anywhere, even in the desert. It can come from intense rainstorms dropping huge amounts of water in a very short time. Flash floods can happen with little or no warning and can reach their peak in only a few minutes. What could make the situation worse is the condition of the ground. If it is already saturated, more water cannot sink in. If the ground is rocky, as it is in some mountains and canyons, barely any water at all can be absorbed by the land.

One of the worst flash floods in history occurred in July 1976 in the Colorado Rocky Mountains.

THE BIG THOMPSON FLOOD

It is estimated that there were about 3,000 people in the Thompson River Canyon that Saturday. People in campers and cabins along the Big Thompson River at the bottom of the canyon were celebrating this special weekend. It was Colorado's state centennial.

On Saturday evening a thunderstorm pummeled the canyon for three hours. Up to twelve inches of rain fell on the rocky slopes of the canyon. Because there was not enough soil to soak up such a heavy rainfall, the river water rose.

A nineteen-foot wall of water built up and roared down the Big Thompson River dragging everything in its path with it, including trees, big boulders, camping equipment, pieces of cabins—and even a whole building not yet broken apart.

One hundred and forty people lost their lives in Big Thompson Canyon that day. Eight hundred people were stranded on top of the canyon walls. Also destroyed were 316 homes, fifty-six mobile homes, and fifty-two businesses.

Today, all along the canyon roads, you can see signs that urge people to abandon their cars and climb to safety at the first sign of a flash flood.

Dam failures can result in the worst type of flash flood. When a dam fails, a gigantic amount of water is descends upon an area, often with devastating consequences. One

> **Did You Know?**
>
> Just six inches of moving water can knock a person down. A mere two feet of water can float a large bus. The greatest and most dangerous mistake people make is not abandoning their cars when they are stalled in flood waters.

of the worst flash floods from heavy rain and dam failure occurred in Johnstown, Pennsylvania, in 1889.

The Johnstown Flood

Dams are built to control water. They may be built to create a lake or to keep certain lands from flooding. A dam was built in the Appalachian Mountains above the industrial town of Johnstown, Pennsylvania. It was a prosperous place in 1889. New families were moving in. New businesses and factories were being created. It was a time before telephones and a time when people still used horses to get around.

There had been some flooding in the past, but the people of Johnstown were used to that. They lived where two rivers meet and spring flooding was a natural occurrence. People did what they always did. They moved their things to the second floor of their houses. They moved their businesses to the top of their buildings.

On May 30, despite some water still in the streets, the citizens were looking forward to the Memorial Day celebration. That night, heavy rains fell. People moved their belongings to their upper floors. They were ready to wait out the flood.

On the morning of May 31, there was activity and commotion up in the mountains at the South Fork Dam fourteen miles above Johnstown. The South Fork Dam held back Lake Conemaugh, a body of water about two miles long and a mile wide. At three o'clock in the afternoon the dam gave way. Water plunged down the mountain dragging with it houses, trees, people, and animals. Before it was over, 2,209 people would lose their lives.

Down in Johnstown the people had no idea what was coming—until they heard the roar. A rolling hill of debris and water about forty feet high and a half mile wide pounded over them and their town as people scrambled to higher ground for safety.

Six-year-old Gertrude Quinn got separated from her family. As flood waters swirled around her, Gertrude was in trouble. In what must have been a miracle, the little girl landed on a muddy mattress that would be her raft. She held on tight. A house with about twenty people on the roof raced by. Gertrude stretched her arms out to them, but they couldn't catch her. Finally, a man jumped on Gertrude's mattress to help her. He and Gertrude hung on and together went downstream. Gertrude and her family were reunited that very day.

The Johnstown Flood went down in history as one of the worst floods of all time.

But the town's people worked hard and restored the city. Help poured in from all over the country—food and medicine and offers to rebuild homes. Everyone pulled together and Johnstown was rebuilt.

5

Other Types of Floods

The four main kinds of floods are river floods, flash floods, ice jams, and coastal floods. Within each group, there are different sets of conditions that create variations.

Coastal Flooding

It happens in every state that touches the Atlantic or the Pacific oceans. Coastal flooding occurs when ocean waters come up over land. Severe storms that bring huge waves and elevated water levels are usually the reason.

Over the centuries, California's people have built seawalls to protect their homes and towns. These walls reduce the strength and impact of ocean waves and prevent the washing away of sand beaches.

Some of the greatest coastal flooding comes in the fall, winter, and early months of spring in the form of a nor'easter. These storms bring heavy snow or rain, coastal flooding, and strong winds from the northeast, for which they are named. States from Florida through Maine can be affected. In some cases, electricity is lost and towns need to be evacuated.

Coastal flooding almost always occurs with hurricanes. High winds and waves slam into coastal towns, ripping down trees and buildings and dragging homes out to sea.

> **Did You Know?**
>
> The California shoreline is constantly changing because of coastal **erosion**. Rough seas, high tides, heavy rainfall, earthquakes, and landslides can all contribute to the changing shoreline.

Tsunami

Picture this. It's a summer night. You've anchored your fishing boat off the coast of Alaska. You're about to go to sleep when your boat starts shaking uncontrollably. Earthquake! It feels like a bad one. Then you see it, a huge wave coming toward you at about one hundred miles an hour. The wave lifts your boat to the top of its crest. You struggle to hold on to the sides as you look down from eighty feet in the air. Your boat crashes down. You manage to get into your skiff, a small flat-bottomed boat you have tied up at the side, and you are rescued later, but it takes a while.

This is what happened to fishermen in

the summer of 1958 in Lituya Bay, Alaska. This huge wave is called a *tsunami*, a Japanese word meaning "harbor wave."

A tsunami is an extreme wave that creates coastal flooding. This ocean wave doesn't crash on shore very often, but when it does, it can cause considerable damage. Tsunamis may occur near Alaska, Hawaii, and other parts of the northwest coast. Tsunamis are most often caused by earthquakes or landslides deep in the middle of the ocean. This sea wave can also be caused by a volcanic eruption, a nuclear explosion, and even meteorites from outer space.

A tsunami is made up of circular waves spreading out from its center in ever-widening circles. It is difficult to see a tsunami in the middle of the ocean. A tsunami can travel unnoticed at about 550 miles an hour—the speed of a jet airplane. It can move from one side of the Pacific Ocean to the other in one day.

When a tsunami nears shore, it can build up tremendous force and a height of fifty to one hundred feet. When a wave of this size hits the coast it can race one thousand feet inland before it rushes back out to sea carrying with it everything in its wake.

> **Did You Know?**
>
> Some people mistakenly call a tsunami a tidal wave. A tsunami is caused by an earthquake or some other disturbance in the ocean. Tidal waves, on the other hand, are caused primarily by the force of gravity from the moon.

6

Real Safety/Real People
Real Safety Tips

What should you do when you hear that a flood or any other natural disaster is about to happen? Turn to *The Weather Channel* or your local radio station for the most accurate and up-to-date information about the problems in your area.

Flood Warning! What to Do:

If no evacuation has been ordered:

- Make sure a battery-powered radio is nearby.

- Collect your Family Disaster Supplies Kit, blankets and sleeping bags, and keep them with you.

- Call your family's emergency contact person to report your plans.

- All children and pets should stay indoors.

- Make sure you have cash and a car with a full tank of gas in case you need to evacuate.

- Obey advisories you hear on television or on the radio.

Immediately before the flood:

- Bring in any outdoor items but do not walk in flood water to get them.

- If you are not at home, go to high ground.

- For sanitary use, in case the water

supply becomes contaminated, thoroughly clean bathtubs with bleach and then fill them with water.

- Place all valuables and family/medical records in waterproof containers and store them on the highest floor of your house.

If evacuation is advised:

- Turn off water and electric utilities.

- Lock windows and doors before leaving home.

- Tune your car radio to news stations with updates on evacuation routes.

During the flood:

- If on foot, do not attempt to walk through flood waters. Instead, turn around and go directly to higher ground.

- Everyone (including pets) must stay

away from flood waters, storm drains, and sewers.

- If you are in a car, never try to take a shortcut through flooded areas. If your car stalls, immediately abandon it and climb to higher ground.

Surviving a flash flood:

- If you suspect a flash flood is about to happen, immediately climb to higher ground.

- Remember, it doesn't have to be raining for a flash flood to occur. Some of the most dangerous floods originate many miles away.

Giving and Getting Help

Kids in floods and other disasters need to know they are not alone. You can help. Messages from other kids mean a lot. If you have been in a flood, you can write to others telling them you know how they feel.

You can also work with your family and your school to help gather canned goods and other food for nearby shelters. You can collect blankets and warm clothing. Sometimes money is collected, too. Every penny helps. Ask your parents and teachers for other ideas.

Using the Internet

The Weather Channel home page has news about floods and other weather-related disasters. The Web site makes information available so that people can be prepared for all weather systems. You can learn a lot about ordinary weather on this home page.

The Weather Channel home page can be found at:

http://www.weather.com

The Weather Channel safety home page can be found at:

http://www.weather.com/safeside/

While you're on the Internet, look for "Eye on the World—Violent Planet Page." The pictures are great and the information is really interesting. You can send messages to people in need of help at: Howdy Friend. You Are Not Alone.

This Site can be reached at:

http:///www.iwaynet.net/%7Ekwroejr/violent.html

The Federal Emergency Management Agency, known as FEMA, has a special weather Site for kids at:

http://www.fema.gov/kids/

Real People

Betsey was ten years old in 1997 when the Red River rose up and flooded her town of East Grand Forks, Minnesota. Betsey and her family lived in a house right on the river. Betsey kept a journal during the flood. Here are her entries. They start when Betsey's family begins to understand that the water might come inside their home.

Friday April 11

We started moving things from the main floor to our second floor. I'm getting nervous.

Sunday April 13

Today the National Guard man came and told us we had to leave by Wednesday. I saw him coming. I am really nervous. Our living room is almost empty now. It still has a couch, a chair, and a grandfather clock.

Tuesday April 15

Today I was sitting on my mom and dad's bed. I was looking out the window at the water coming up the dike. I knew pretty soon we would have to leave our house.

Wednesday April 16

Today we left our house. Before we left we went in our backyard. We stood on the dike. The dike is ten feet high. The water was up to seven feet. No one put sandbags on the dike by our house yet. I felt scared and worried. I didn't know what to do. My mom and dad and my brother Michael and I moved to my grandma's. My brother Tyler and my sister Gina moved into Tyler's girlfriend's house.

Thursday April 17
My mom picked me up after school. We went straight to our house. She said she had to sandbag. Everyone was filling sandbags and piling them on the dike. My dad said he had to stay and help, too. We walked to the car to go to my grandma's. In the car I just started to cry.

Friday April 18
During school a fourth-grade teacher had to leave because water was coming in her house. After school Michael and I went to our grandma's. We helped my grandma bring stuff up from her basement. But then we had to evacuate my grandma's house, too. We went to my uncle's in Crookston, thirty miles away. We were nine people in a two-bedroom house. On the TV they said a mandatory evacuation was on for Grand Forks and East Grand Forks. We never got

to go back to our house to live.

Saturday April 19

Today I was in shock. We went to the evacuation center to register. That's so people would know where we were. Thousands of people came through there in a couple of days.

I don't know what I have left or if I had anything left. Then we moved in with some friends in Crookston. They are so nice to us. And so giving. It is unbelievable.

A year after the flood

During the flood I felt many different things. I was so sad because I lost my house. Water had destroyed everything on the first floor. Our house had to be torn down. I had a very empty feeling whenever I would go by the old lot where my house used to be. We moved to another part of East Grand Forks but I miss my old neighborhood. I miss living near my best friend Carissa. We had so much fun down on the river with her and the other people.

Gregory was twelve years old when the Mississippi River destroyed his town of Valmeyer, Illinois, during the Great Flood of 1993. But a large number of Valmeyer families were not going to let the river take their town away from them. They were a community. They would stick together. Gregory explains what happened:

After the waters receded, there was all kinds of mud and muck. Everything was dead. People came from all over the country to help us clean up our town. Then we found out that it was not possible to resume life as it had been. This meant that the people of our town would have to disband and that families would have to relocate and rebuild in surrounding communities. Valmeyer was a small town, and the kind of town where everybody knows everybody. Relocating to different commu-

nities was the last thing many people wanted to do.

Then the idea to relocate the whole town came into view. Most people fell in love with this idea but there were some skeptics. The community then found a spot up on the bluffs just a half mile east of our former town. This spot was about 1000 feet higher, so there was no threat for a future Mississippi River flood.

Much planning went into this new community. First we planned the streets, where the houses would go, and then the school. Then construction began. We now have a bank, a school, a restaurant, a convenience store, and a park.

The town of Valmeyer is once again a happy place to live, where everybody knows everybody, and everybody is friendly. For me, that's the meaning of community. It's the greatest thing in the world that our community could stick together through all of this hardship.

GLOSSARY

ATMOSPHERE—The mass of gases and particles that extends several hundred miles above Earth. Weather is produced in the six miles closest to the earth.

BLIZZARD—A blinding snowstorm with strong winds, low visibility, and typically severe cold temperatures.

CREST—The highest water level a river reaches before it recedes.

DEBRIS—The scattered remains of something broken or destroyed.

DIKE—A wall or embankment of earth and stone built to prevent floods.

EROSION—A gradual wearing away caused by wind, water, and waves.

FLASH FLOOD—A flood that occurs suddenly, typically produced by heavy rainfall in a short amount of time.

FLOODPLAIN—The land surrounding rivers which fills with water when the rivers overflow.

GROUNDWATER—Water that fills the spaces and cracks below the earth's surface.

NATURAL DISASTER—Any disaster caused by forces of nature such as floods, tornadoes, hurricanes, and earthquakes.

PRECIPITATION—Water that falls from the atmosphere and reaches the ground, such as rain, snow, or sleet.

SANDBAGS—Small bags filled with sand and used to raise and reinforce dikes.

SATURATION—Point at which no more liquid can be absorbed.

TRIBUTARIES—Rivers that flow into one main river, such as the Ohio and Missouri which flow into the main river, the Mississippi.

VAPOR—The gaseous state of a substance that is usually liquid like water or solid like ice.

INDEX

Army Corps of Engineers 37
atmosphere 17

Big Thompson River 39

coastal flooding 45
creeks, expanding to rivers 28

East Grand Forks, Minnesota 11
Emergency Animal Rescue Service 12
evacuation 8

factors causing floods:
   weather 18
   ground 21
   people 24
Family Disaster Supply Kit 51
Federal Emergency Management Agency (FEMA) 55
floodplain 25

Grand Forks Herald, The 14
Grand Forks, North Dakota 8

Great Flood of 1997 8
groundwater 21

Humane Society 12

ice-jam floods 29

Johnstown Flood 41

Minnesota River 10
Mississippi River Basin 30

National Guard 13
National Weather Service 9

Red River 8

saturation 21
snow fleas 30

tsunami 47

Valmeyer, Illinois 59

water cycle 19
Weather Channel, The 50
Web sites 54-55